TECHNOLOGY IN ACTION

TRAIN TECHNOLOGY

Michael Pollard

Titles in this series

Aircraft Technology

Car Technology

Spacecraft Technology

TV and Video Technology

Ship Technology

Train Technology

First published in 1989
Wayland (Publishers) Ltd
61 Western Road, Hove
East Sussex BN3 1JD, England

©Copyright 1989 Wayland (Publishers) Ltd

Edited by Jollands Editions
Designed by Alison Anholt-White

British Library Cataloguing in Publication Data
Pollard, Michael, *1931–*
    Train technology
    1. Trains
    I. Title. II. Series
    625.2

    ISBN 1-85210-819-3

Typeset by Direct Image Photosetting Limited,
Sussex, England
Printed in Italy by G. Canale & C.S.p.A., Turin
Bound in France by A.G.M.

Front cover The French TGV high speed train holds the world speed record
at 409 kph.

Contents

There have been three stages in the development of railways. The first stage was from about 1830 to 1930. This was a time of growth in every country, when most of the great railways of the world were built.

Railways grew out of the need to haul heavy loads such as coal and building stone. Only after the first lines had been built did the railway companies realise that carrying passengers could also be profitable. Technologies gradually developed which enabled locomotives to haul heavy loads at high speeds, and allowed large numbers of trains to use the network of tracks in safety. These basic technologies have since been improved or replaced.

In the second stage, from about 1930 to 1970, the railways were allowed to decline in many countries, due to the fact that road transport was becoming cheaper and more efficient. During this time, thousands of kilometres of track were closed, and many people said that rail travel would soon be a thing of the past.

The third stage of railway development, from 1970, proved this forecast wrong. Especially in towns and cities, road travel had become a problem. With so many vehicles using fuel from oil, there were worries that the world's oil supplies would not last for ever. Also, the exhaust gases from millions of road vehicles were increasing pollution in the world's cities.

The Gare de Lyon in Paris, France. In the background is a high speed train, known in France as the TGV *(Train à Grande Vitesse)*. TGVs often reach a speed of 275 kph or more.

The railways began to fight back. Using new technology, faster and more efficient trains were built. In some countries, special tracks were laid to carry the new high speed trains. New methods of controlling railway traffic meant that tracks could be used more heavily and so more profitably. It was soon realised that the best way of transporting large numbers of people was to use fast passenger trains. At the same time, the railways were able to speed up the movement of freight trains which had previously been very slow.

Railway technology draws very much on the past. The old technology based on steam power has been replaced in most countries, but it led to the development of methods of operation which are still used. To understand today's signalling systems, for example, we have to look at how they developed out of the systems of the past. Meanwhile, advancing technology is beginning to equip the world's railways for the twenty-first century.

Above A replica of the *Rocket*, which was built by George Stephenson in 1829.

Below A steam locomotive seen climbing on the famous Darjeeling – Himalaya Railway. The 88 km journey takes over seven hours to complete.

In the early days of steam locomotion, trains with their large wheels often became derailed on bends. One invention to solve this problem, Prosser's patent guide wheels (illustrated here), was unsuccessful. By the mid-nineteenth century, most locomotives had bogie wheels in front that swivelled freely.

Building and operating the railways in the nineteenth century called for skills which had never before been needed on such a large scale. Much of the technology had to be developed from the beginning. Unlike horse-drawn transport, trains could not climb steep hills or go round sharp bends.

Never before had so much earth been moved to make cuttings and embankments. Never before had so many bridges or tunnels been built. No one had ever tried to build roads across some of the wild country where railways went. Surveyors and engineers had to solve problems as they went along.

The track itself had to be laid down to exact measurements and stand up to punishing treatment from heavily-laden trains. Sometimes the track was laid over marshy land or across sand, and the ground beneath the track had to be specially prepared.

The development of the steam locomotive made railways possible. In the 1820s, steam engines had been in use in coal mines, to drive water pumps, for over 100 years. But these were stationary engines used to drive fixed machinery. Putting a steam engine on wheels and using it to haul a load was the breakthrough that began the railway age.

As railways developed, the need for new skills and technology grew. Often, accidents revealed new problems that needed to be solved. This was especially true of signalling methods. The increasing speed and weight of trains meant that new, more efficient braking systems had to be developed. Meanwhile, the design of steam locomotives improved until, in the 1930s, it reached a peak of power and efficiency with such locomotives as the London and North Eastern Railway's *Mallard* in Britain and the Union Pacific's Big Boys in the USA.

Technology brought increased comfort for passengers too. At first, it was speed that attracted people to use the railways. Later, they demanded more comfort – and technology came to their aid by improving the suspension of passenger carriages, and adding lighting and heating. Even the problems of cooking and serving food on board a moving train were solved.

Space exploration has provided much of the spur to today's technology, in computer development, for example. In a similar way, for most of the nineteenth century it was the railways that were at the forefront of new ideas.

The interior of a dining car on the Trans-Siberian Railway. This railway is the longest in the world and covers a distance of almost 10,000 km. The journey from Moscow to Vladivostok takes about eight days. This remarkable railway is electrified over most of the route. Apart from regular passenger services, there is heavy freight movement with containers from the Far East to all parts of Europe as the main traffic.

The first railways were built with iron rails spiked or clipped to wooden cross-ties (called 'sleepers' in Britain) and laid on a bed of stone chippings called ballast. As locomotives became more powerful and could pull heavier loads, wear on the iron rails became a problem. From about 1860 iron was replaced by steel. This was more expensive at first, but as steel rails lasted longer it led to savings later on. In recent years, wooden sleepers have largely been replaced in Britain – though not in other countries where wood is more plentiful – by concrete. This has made the repair and laying of track a speedier and more efficient process.

Maintaining the track in good condition is vital, but expensive. In the past, when wages were low, large gangs of workers were employed to inspect, repair and re-lay track. This was one reason why rails were made in short lengths of about 30 metres that were not too difficult for a gang of workers to handle.

In many countries it is now too expensive to employ so many people on track laying and maintenance, and the work is done by machines operated by only a few workers. This also has the advantage that the work is done more quickly, and with less interruption to rail traffic.

A French National Railways (SNCF) high speed train at speed around a curve on the track between Paris and Lyons. The track is raised or banked on the outside causing the train to lean inwards in the same way as a motorcyclist going round a bend at speed. Note the closely-spaced sleepers.

There are many different methods. Sometimes complete sections of track, with the rails already fixed to concrete ties, are made up in the factory and transported to the site. Then they are laid in position by crane, and the rails are welded together. Another method, used in Australia, is to use a series of machines. The first lays lengths of welded rail by the side of the track. A second machine follows up with the cross-ties, and a third lifts the rails into their final position and spikes them.

In Japan, France and Britain, a method called 'slab-track' or Paved Concrete Track (PACT for short) is sometimes used. This does away with the need for ballast and cross-ties. A 'paving train' lays two slabs of concrete. The top layer has clips for the rails already in place. A track-laying vehicle follows up the 'paving train' with the rails. 'Slab-track' is laid more quickly than normal track on a ballast bed, and it is easier and cheaper to maintain.

In some countries such as France, Italy and Japan, high speed trains – those that travel in excess of 160 kph over long distances – run on track specially built for high speed use (see page 33).

The PACT or 'slab-track' unit lays a continuous concrete track-bed about 30 cm thick, completing about 40 metres per hour. When the concrete is dry, a track-laying vehicle follows up and clips the rails in place.

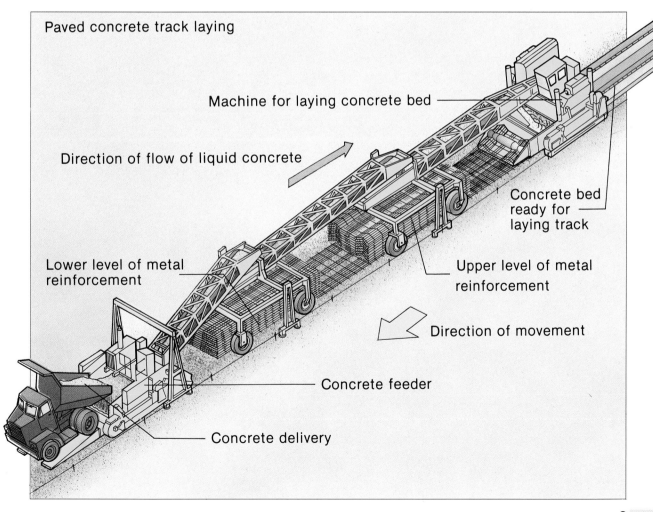

Paved concrete track laying

Machine for laying concrete bed

Direction of flow of liquid concrete

Concrete bed ready for laying track

Lower level of metal reinforcement

Upper level of metal reinforcement

Direction of movement

Concrete feeder

Concrete delivery

The early railway builders had to work within very strict limits. The first steam locomotives had very little power and could not climb gradients at speed with a load behind them. The track had to be built as near level as possible. Cuttings and embankments were used to take lines through quite low ranges of hills. This greatly increased the cost of building railways, but it helped in the development of a technology for earth-moving. At first, earth was moved by men and barrows, but later steam-powered excavators called steam-shovels – the ancestors of the modern bulldozer – were used to do the work.

Within a few years, more powerful locomotives were being built. Gradients became less of a problem except in really mountainous country. By 1860 it was possible to build a line through the Rocky Mountains of North America, with gradients that no locomotive could have climbed twenty years before. The railways in the Scottish Highlands were all built after 1860, and locomotives were so powerful by this time that not a single tunnel was needed to carry the line through the hills and mountains.

In mountainous country such as parts of North America and central Europe, the railway-builders had to overcome the problem of crossing wide rivers and deep valleys. In the Rocky Mountains of the United States and Canada, they made use of 'trestle' bridges, built on the spot with the wood that was freely available. Railway building led to a surge in bridge technology.

One of the great bridge-builders of the time was Alexandre Eiffel, the designer of the Eiffel Tower in Paris. He made his name, however, as a designer of railway bridges in difficult country.

His most famous work was the Garabit Viaduct high in the mountains of central France.

A double-headed diesel-electric Amtrak passenger train winds its way through the mountains north of Los Angeles, California. Laying an east-west railway track through the mountains of North America was an incredible achievement. Hundreds of cuttings such as this one had to be blasted out of the rock before the track could be laid.

It crossed a 165-metre wide valley at a height of 146 metres. The great problem here was the strength of the winds that funnelled up the valley. Eiffel set up weather stations to measure the wind, and designed the viaduct with a specially wide base to keep it stable. Wind resistance was reduced by building the viaduct of open girders, with latticework sides to protect trains passing over. The viaduct, completed in 1884, survives – but despite Eiffel's precautions trains were allowed to use it only at restricted speeds. This experience led Eiffel to study winds more closely, and to build the first wind tunnel for test purposes.

The Garabit Viaduct, built by Alexandre Gustave Eiffel in the mountains of central France. In the construction of arched bridges, the arch can either be below the track or above it, as in the case of the Sydney Harbour Bridge in Australia.

When railways began, steam was the only mechanical source of power. Steam locomotives used the cheapest fuel available. In Britain and Western Europe, this was coal, which was plentiful. In North America it was wood from the forests.

In the boiler of a steam engine, huge pressures of steam build up. If this pressure becomes too high, a safety valve allows some of the steam to escape into the air.

The first locomotives were often expected to pull heavier loads than they were designed for. To build up steam pressure, the drivers would often screw down the safety valve so that it did not work. Frequently, the result of this action was a boiler explosion.

This was what happened to *The Best Friend of Charleston*, the first steam locomotive built in the USA. In 1831, after it had been in service for five months, the driver screwed down the safety valve to gain more power. The boiler blew up and he was killed. There were many such accidents until a British engineer, John Ramsbottom, invented a safety valve that the driver could not tamper with. At about the same time, boilers began to be made of steel instead of the weaker iron.

In the first 100 years of railways, companies raced against each other to build locomotives which could pull heavier and heavier loads at faster and faster speeds. But the more powerful locomotives became, the more fuel they used and so the more expensive they were to run.

Engineers invented two ways of cutting fuel costs. One was the compound locomotive. In this design, the steam was used twice to provide

This early American locomotive has two distinguishing features: a large funnel to prevent sparks from starting prairie fires, and a cow-catcher in front.

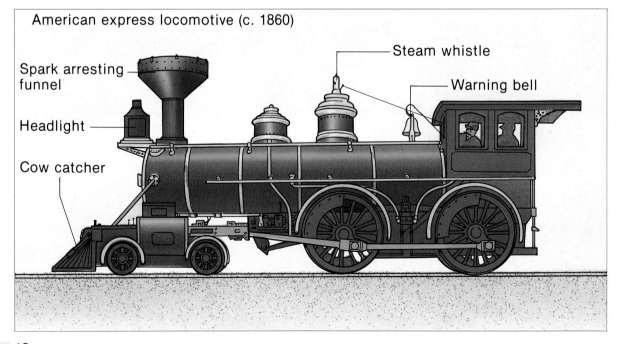

American express locomotive (c. 1860)

Spark arresting funnel

Headlight

Cow catcher

Steam whistle

Warning bell

A Chinese freight train being hauled by two large steam locomotives of modern manufacture. As yet, China has less electrified track than most other countries, and relies largely on steam and diesel locomotives. The heavy freight locomotive shown in the picture is of recent Chinese manufacture.

power to the driving wheels before being discharged through the funnel. Around 1900 a new idea boosted fuel savings even more. This was called superheating. Once the steam had been made in the boiler, it was passed into tubes where it was made even hotter. This superheated steam expanded and so provided more energy for the driving wheels.

Even these new ideas, however, could not save steam power. In the most efficient steam locomotive, only about eight per cent of the energy produced by the fuel is used. The rest is wasted. In 1879, the first electric locomotive was built in Germany, and in 1892 the diesel engine was invented. These two developments were to revolutionize railways all over the world.

Live wires and rails

In the last half of the nineteenth century, cities in Europe and North America grew as new suburbs were built around them. The population of New York, for example, doubled between 1780 and 1880. One result of this was the need for rapid transit systems to carry people between the suburbs and city centres to work. Train services had to be fast, punctual, reliable, and able to pick up passengers at stations only a few kilometres apart.

Steam-hauled trains were unsuitable for this work. Where the city tracks needed to run underground, the problems of ventilating long tunnels could not be overcome. Steam locomotives also take a long time to build up speed, and the fuel used to do this is wasted if they have to stop frequently. The answer for trains running across cities, whether overland or underground, and for services to the suburbs was electric traction.

An electric locomotive operated by the German State Railways (DB). This type of locomotive draws its power from overhead cables connected with the grid system. It does this by means of a pantograph, which in its simplest form is a spring-loaded, diamond-shaped frame with copper or carbon contact strip. One advantage of this system compared with the third rail is that of safety.

No better way has been found of moving large numbers of people in and around cities, and new rapid transit systems using electric traction are still being built. These systems usually use rails – either the track rails or a special 'third rail' – to supply electricity to the train motors. The trains, accelerating and braking quickly, can be operated close together in safety, and need less maintenance than steam or diesel locomotives. In most systems the traction unit forms part of the leading coach, and the trains are operated in 'sets' of four or six coaches which can be doubled up to carry heavy rush hour traffic.

Electric motors are reliable and, of course, do not have to carry their fuel with them. The disadvantage of electricity is that it is expensive to install and maintain. For this reason, it is used only for the busiest rail lines. It would not be worth the cost of electrifying the great trans-continental routes of North America or Asia, for example. These are run more cheaply using diesel locomotives.

Outside city areas, the electricity is usually carried on overhead cables and collected by pantographs. These are collectors mounted on top of the traction unit and held against the overhead wires by springs. This system, with the live wires safely out of reach, allows higher voltages to be used and so heavy loads can be hauled at high speeds.

An advantage of electric traction in today's world, where the need to preserve our environment is so important, is that it is clean.

Above In the Paris Metro and most other underground railway systems, the 'third rail' on the track supplies power to the train's motors. An overhead system would call for high tunnels.

Left Tramcars, as seen here in Basle, Switzerland, are still operating in many of the world's cities. Although these date back to the very early days of public transport, it is possible that this system may be revived as a means of rapid transport in large cities.

Railway engineers have always looked for more efficient and less expensive ways of hauling trains. Especially in countries with no coal of their own, the invention of the diesel engine, burning oil, looked like the answer.

The first diesel-powered locomotives were built round about 1900 and were used in shunting yards. They were not powerful enough to haul complete trains. But engineers soon went on to design more powerful diesel locomotives. The first diesel-hauled rail service began in Sweden in 1913, with a diesel engine mounted in the front part of a passenger coach. Diesel railcars, as they were called, were later used in many countries. The power produced by the engine was transmitted to the driving wheels by way of gears and a clutch, as they are in a diesel-engined road vehicle.

This method of transmission was satisfactory for railcars, but not for locomotives to haul heavy passenger or freight trains. It did not give enough power. The answer was to make the diesel engine drive another power unit which then transmitted its power to the wheels. Engineers in the USA led the world in the development of the diesel-electric locomotive, in which the engine drives an electric generator whose power turns the wheels. This gives the locomotive the advantages of smooth running and extra power when it is needed to climb steep gradients or pull extra-heavy loads. Diesel-electric locomotives built by the

A diesel-electric locomotive uses diesel fuel to drive a generator, and this makes electricity to give power to the motors. Diesel-electrics are ideal for heavy freight work on lines too remote to justify the cost of electrification. They can be doubled up to provide extra motive power for long trains.

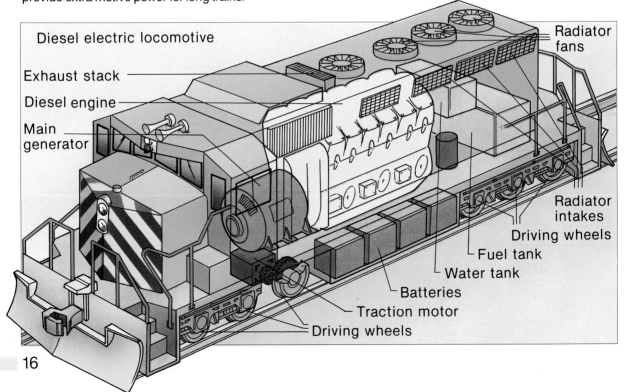

Diesel electric locomotive
Exhaust stack
Diesel engine
Main generator
Radiator fans
Radiator intakes
Driving wheels
Fuel tank
Water tank
Batteries
Traction motor
Driving wheels

In the USA, the National Railroad Passenger Corporation, generally known as Amtrak, provides a passenger service over the whole national rail network. Diesel-electrics are widely used for this purpose. These can be doubled up or run in threes or more thereby providing a very powerful traction unit.

American General Electric and General Motors companies are in use in many countries throughout the world.

In another type of diesel locomotive, the diesel engine drives an oil pump which turns the blades of a turbine. This is called diesel-hydraulic traction.

In the search for a super-efficient locomotive, engineers have also tried using gas turbines similar to those used in aircraft. In a 'turbo-train' the turbine drives an electric generator, as in the diesel-electric system, which transmits power to the wheels. Turbo-trains have been tried out in many countries, and are still used in Canada for example. But the high hopes engineers had for them proved false. When running at full power they are very efficient, so they are best used over long distances with heavy loads. On shorter journeys or with smaller loads they are more expensive to run than diesel-electrics.

It was the idea of the track along which trains could run that made railways possible. But some new ideas on railways do away with rails altogether.

One reason for this is that maintaining the track in good condition is very costly. Another is that the friction between the wheels and the rails not only damages them but also restricts speed. Icy weather causes problems for trains collecting electricity from the rails, because icing prevents the current from passing to the collector shoes.

One idea for 'railways without rails' is the maglev (MAGnetic LEVitation) train. The track is a line of permanent magnets which attract electromagnets in the train as it passes over them. The electromagnets switch on and off to control the train's speed.

No part of the train touches the track. The two sets of magnets are always a few millimetres apart. As a result, there is no friction and maglevs can run at up to 500 kph. As they are electric, there is no pollution, and as there is no contact with the track there is no noise.

Maglevs sound like a good idea for the future, but there are snags. One is that the maglev track is expensive to build. Another is that no one has yet worked out a way of switching a maglev train from one track to another. So far, maglevs can only run direct from one place to another, with no junctions. An example is the maglev that runs between Birmingham Airport in England and the nearby National Exhibition Centre.

Another idea that has been tried out is the hovertrain. This works in the same way as a hovercraft, held up on a cushion of air. In the 1970s the French engineering company Bertin built a special track to take a hovertrain, which they called the 'Aerotrain'. The experiment was not successful. One problem was that the

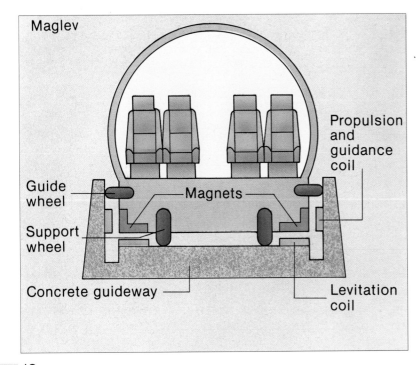

Maglev · Propulsion and guidance coil · Guide wheel · Magnets · Support wheel · Concrete guideway · Levitation coil

For direct, place to place travel with no branching lines, the maglev (magnetic levitation) could be the train of the future. The train when running is raised a few millimetres above the line by the action of very powerful magnets repelling each other. At the same time, it is propelled forward by a linear induction motor. This acts like a flattened and elongated electric motor.

Aerotrain was, like all hovercraft, very noisy. But it may be that when some of the problems are overcome the hovertrain will be tried again.

In the meantime, engineers have turned to ways of improving speed, efficiency and comfort on more conventional track. The technology to design and produce maglevs and hovertrains is available, but the practical problems of operating them satisfactorily have still to be solved.

Right At present, maglev systems are largely experimental and are only operated over short distances. The track is costly to build but needs little maintenance. Maglev trains are quiet, smooth and cause absolutely no pollution.

Below Many countries are experimenting with maglev trains, including the USA, Canada, Japan, Britain and West Germany. Maglevs can run very fast and a Japanese model has achieved speeds in excess of 500 kph.

Trains cannot swerve to avoid each other. If they are running on the same track they must be kept well apart. When trains are travelling at speed they take a long time to slow down or stop.

From the beginning, railway companies saw that a signalling system was needed to show drivers whether the track ahead was clear. The first signalmen stood by the line and stopped trains or waved them on with their arms or with flags, using lamps at night. Each set of points was controlled by a man with a lever which he pulled to switch a train to the correct track.

Human signals were soon replaced by various kinds of visual signals using discs, boards, metal arms or, in North America, balls hoisted on tall masts.

In the early days, trains were kept apart by time intervals. Signals stopped a train until five minutes after the train in front had passed. This system failed if the first train broke down or was delayed for other reasons. Another problem was that the system depended on clocks or watches which did not always agree.

After a series of terrible accidents, signalling technology gradually changed, from about 1840, to the 'block' method of working which is still used today. A block is a length of track which must be occupied by only one train at a time. A train may enter a block only if the signal controlling it shows that it is safe to do so.

In this traditional Swiss signal box the signalman has to use considerable strength to set signals and points with one movement of the lever.

An old-style British signal box showing the heavy wheel for opening and closing the level-crossing.

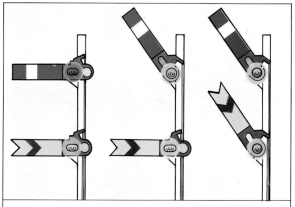

Semaphore signals set at (left) Danger–stop; (centre) Go, but with caution; (right) All clear.

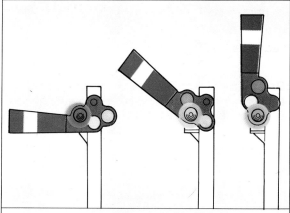

The arm of this semaphore signal moves to the diagonal for 'proceed with caution' and to the vertical for 'all clear'.

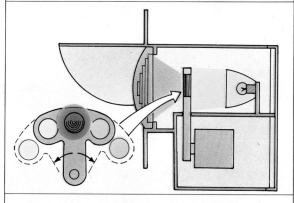

Modern colour light signals. The amber light warns that the next signal is red.

The telegraph, invented in 1837, made block working possible. The signalmen for each block could send messages to each other, using a bell code. By this time, signals and points were operated by wires from signal-boxes. The signalman for one block would 'offer' a train to the next box down the line by bell. The second signalman would 'accept' the train if his own block was clear. This system was a great improvement, but safety still depended on the signalmen. They might forget to set a signal at danger, or to set the points correctly for an approaching train.

From about 1860 onwards a new safety device was introduced. This was called 'interlocking' and enabled a signalman to set both signals and points with one movement of a lever. There was now no danger that a train would be switched on to the wrong track or be derailed by a set of open points. But the biggest safety improvement, which is the basis of all railway signalling today, had still to come.

The main purpose of signalling is to ensure safety, but modern systems can also help to provide punctual and frequent services, especially on crowded lines, by allowing the track to be used to its fullest capacity.

The basis of modern systems is the track circuit. This enables the signals to be set by the trains themselves as they move from one block to the next. As well as the red or green light signals controlling entry to each block, distant signals, showing one or two amber lights, warn the driver if he needs to slow down because of red signals further on. The track circuit also operates any crossing gates in the next block.

A modern signal-box can control many kilometres of track including sidings, points, stations and crossings. In some boxes the route map of the area is shown on visual display units like television screens, sometimes backed up with screens showing the actual scene at important spots. The signalman feeds in signal and points changes using a keyboard. In others, the route map is displayed on a track diagram on which lights show the state of the signals and points, and the position of trains in the system.

The networks of tracks around large cities

Below The track circuit has been the basis of railway signalling on busy lines for a century. The wheels of the train short-circuit the track-circuit current and de-activate the relay. This changes the lights behind the train to red.

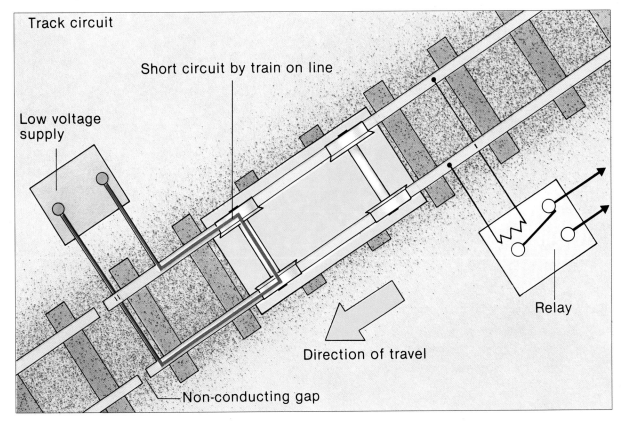

Track circuit

Short circuit by train on line

Low voltage supply

Relay

Direction of travel

Non-conducting gap

The signal control centre for a goods marshalling yard at Zurich, Switzerland. Here freight cars are shunted and sorted continuously. The illuminated track diagram provides an instant picture of all positions and movements. The operator is able to control these by means of switches on the operating console.

may carry trains from a number of different starting stations to various destinations. In some signal-boxes a system called 'entrance-exit' enables the signalman to choose a programmed route for a train by pressing two buttons, one for the entry point and another for the exit. All the signals and points for this route are then set automatically. While it is passing along the route the train is protected from conflicting train movements by a system of interlocking.

The track circuit is an electrical circuit which operates along a block whose rails are insulated from those at each end. A safe low-voltage current passes along one rail, across to the other and back. A switching device called a relay is connected across the rails. When a train enters the block, the current flows through its wheels and cuts out the relay. This switches the block signal to red, operates the distant signal light and indicates the changes on the track diagram in the signal-box. When the train leaves the block, current again flows through the relay and re-sets the signals.

Modern methods of signalling make it almost impossible for a signalman to make a mistake. If he does, checks in the electronic system prevent signals from being set wrongly and so causing a crash. In North America and some European countries, signals tell the driver not only whether to stop or go but also the speed at which he should travel.

But what about the driver? Signals can warn him, but they cannot make him slow down or stop. Especially in fog or snowy weather, signals can be misread or not seen at all.

Most countries now use some kind of automatic train control, at least on their busiest lines. This works from the track circuits. One system gives the driver a warning by bell or horn if he passes a distant warning signal or a signal set at red. The driver has to operate a lever to show that he has heard the warning. If he does not take action to slow down or stop, the brakes come on automatically after a short time as a further safety precaution.

The driving compartment of a class 103 electric locomotive of the German State Railway. The class 103 high speed locomotive has been in service for some years and is capable of a running speed of 200 kph. Maintaining this speed over a long distance places a heavy responsibility on the driver who must be alert at all times.

Automatic train control systems vary from one country, and sometimes from one line, to another. In some systems, the brakes come on slightly as an extra warning to the driver, who must then apply them fully. In others, they bring the train to a stop. On the high speed *Shinkansen* railways of Japan, the speed of the train is controlled automatically all through the journey.

Using electronic controls on the train combined with track circuits it would now be possible to operate trains without drivers. Trains which could be driverless have been running on part of London's Underground system for over twenty years, and, in the USA, on the Metro in Washington DC, and the BART system in San Francisco. Their starting, stopping and speed are all controlled by electrical signals from the track, and the trains operate in complete safety. Any fault in the track, such as a broken rail, breaks the track circuit and stops the train before the danger spot.

However, few people would be very keen to travel on a train without a driver, and so these automatic trains have never been operated, except for test purposes, in that way. Perhaps one day human resistance to the idea of driverless trains will be overcome. After all, lifts in shops and offices once had 'drivers' to operate them, and it was thought that no one would enter a lift without one. Nowadays, we think nothing of 'driving' a lift ourselves.

Above An automatic subway train at Lille in France. This train could be used without a driver so that passengers could use the front of the train as a vantage point.

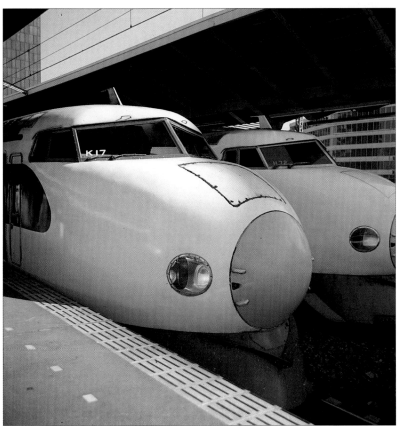

Left The *Shinkansen Hikari*, or lightning trains of Japan travel at a running speed of 210 kph. The streamlined nose contains a computerized driver's compartment, similar to the cockpit of a modern airliner.

It seems surprising today that the companies operating the first railways gave little thought to how their trains could be stopped. To them, speed was the important thing. Some early locomotives could be stopped only by throwing the engine into reverse. Even where locomotives had brakes, these had to provide all the stopping power for the whole train; coaches and goods wagons had no brakes of their own that could be operated while the train was on the move.

When trains began to run at higher speeds, the need for better braking systems became urgent. In 1869 a young American engineer, George Westinghouse, invented the air braking system that became standard throughout the United States and most of the world. In an improved form, it is still used today.

Air brakes are operated by compressed air which forces brake shoes against the wheels when the brake handle or pedal is operated. The compressed air is carried in a pipe which runs the whole length of the train and so can be connected to the brakes of each coach or wagon. Westinghouse's invention greatly increased the stopping power of a train, so that trains could be run safely at higher speeds.

An alternative system, vacuum braking, was used in Britain and some other countries. It too had a continuous pipe along the length of the train. Operation of the brake control created a vacuum which moved the brake shoes.

A new SD 50 diesel locomotive clearly showing the train pipe in the front. This is a flexible, airtight connection between all parts of the train, by means of which either the air or vacuum braking system can be activated from one end of a train to the other.

Both of these systems gave the driver far more control over his train, but they had one disadvantage. If, for any reason, the continuous pipe leaked or broke, the system failed. In 1872 Westinghouse added a 'fail safe' device which applied the brakes automatically throughout the train if the pipe broke. This ended the nightmare of the 'runaway train' that frightened so many rail travellers. A similar device was later introduced for vacuum brakes.

With the changeover in almost every country to diesel or electric locomotives, which have surplus power available to compress air, air brakes have become standard on most rail networks. An extra safety measure is the provision of a chain or handle in passenger coaches which enables a passenger to make a partial application of the brakes in an emergency. This warns the driver, who can then apply the brake fully and stop the train.

The train pipes of an air braking system (top) are filled with compressed air, and more compressed air is stored in the reservoir. When the driver applies the brakes compressed air enters the cylinders and the brakes go on. In the vacuum brake system (below), when brakes are applied, air enters the system to break the vacuum.

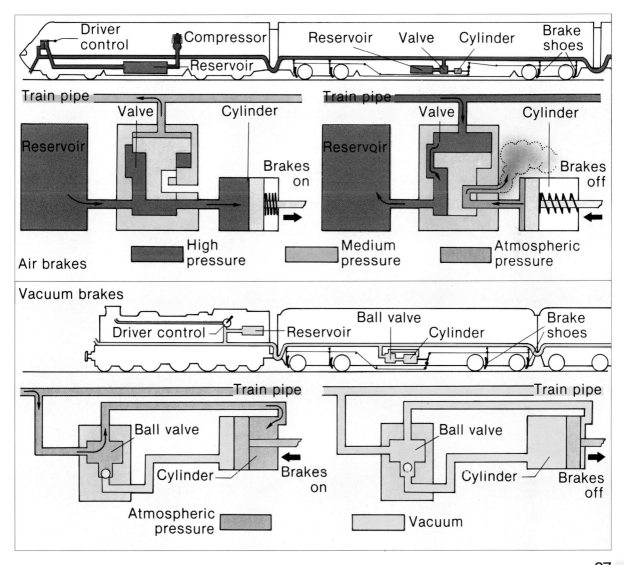

Although passenger trains receive most public attention, the haulage of freight is more important to most railways, except for those in and around cities. Today, many railways have stopped their passenger services and carry only freight. Travel across Australia and North America, for example, is so much faster – and cheaper – by air. For shorter journeys, many people now use their cars.

In the same way, small parcels which used to be sent by rail now go by air or road. This leaves the railways with the job of carrying heavy, bulky loads such as coal, iron ore, grain and building materials. Today's wagons are designed to carry a particular kind of freight and to be loaded or unloaded as quickly as possible.

Illustrated below are just a few of the numerous special purpose freight cars.

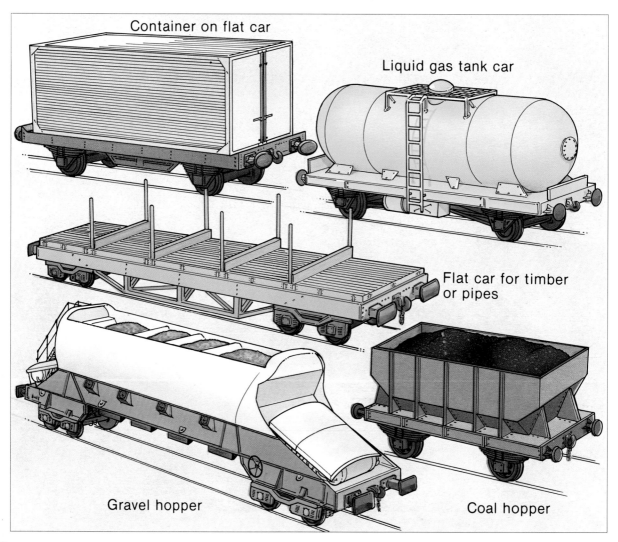

Container on flat car

Liquid gas tank car

Flat car for timber or pipes

Gravel hopper

Coal hopper

Two Canadian Pacific Railway freight trains pass each other in British Columbia.

Many freight trains – such as the 'merry-go-round' trains that carry coal from the mines to power stations in Britain, and the similar operation at Crowsnest Pass in British Columbia – are made up as permanent units. These unit trains are loaded and unloaded automatically and spend their time continually carrying loads of coal over the same route.

Other trains are split up on their journey and individual wagons are sent to different places. This happens with, for example, trains of car transporters which carry cars for a number of different cities. The complicated operation of splitting up trains and sorting out the wagons to make up new trains is done in marshalling yards. In modern yards like those at Alyth near Calgary, and at Conway near Pittsburgh,

computers play an important part. They 'read' the information on the label of each wagon and then switch the points to the siding where it will form part of a new train. The computer can also apply the wagon's brakes so that it comes to rest smoothly. One vital part of the operation still has to be performed by humans, who uncouple the wagons as they pass over the 'hump' which slows them to walking speed.

Saving time is the key to freight train operations. Wagons earn money only when they are full and on the move. The aim of freight handling depots is to load or unload wagons as soon as possible and send them on their way. In the same way, marshalling yards aim for speed in splitting up incoming trains and sending off new ones.

Passengers on a train want three things: to be safe, to arrive on time, and to travel in comfort. They usually have to pay extra for comfort. Since railways began they have divided their passengers into two or more different 'classes'. The first class paid the highest fares and travelled in the greatest comfort. The lowest class passengers were crowded together in poorly-lit, unheated coaches with wooden seats. In the early days, they even used open trucks with no protection from rain and cold.

As the railways grew and people travelled longer distances, they demanded greater comfort. Some of the longest passenger routes were in the USA, and railway companies there went to great lengths to make their passengers comfortable. In 1867 George Pullman of Chicago began to build sleeping and 'parlour' cars which were far more comfortable than anything on European railways, and 'Pullman' soon became the standard for railway comfort everywhere.

The first class refreshment car on a French TGV (Train à Grande Vitesse). The TGV has an operating speed of around 260 kph, but is capable of speeds well in excess. The operations centre in Paris relays the maximum permitted speed direct to an electronic display in the driver's cab throughout the journey.

Below The Indian Palace on Wheels.

Above Passenger comfort on a Finnish train.

Until quite recently rail travel was often dirty and noisy, however soft the seats might be. The designers of modern passenger coaches have taken many ideas from airliners, such as adjustable seats, sound insulation, air conditioning and video entertainment. On many long-distance trains, meals are brought to passengers in their seats, as on aircraft, rather than served in a special dining car.

On shorter journeys, keeping trains on time is more important than comfort. These trains are often crowded, with many passengers standing. The main concern of designers of coaches for these services is that passengers can get on or off quickly so that trains are not held up. Wide gangways and wide automatic sliding doors help to keep stops as short as possible. In some countries commuter trains are made up of double-decker coaches, but these cannot be filled or emptied so quickly.

Another aspect of a comfortable rail journey is making sure that passengers catch their trains and are told about any delays. In recent years there have been great improvements in passenger information. There are computerized displays of train information at important stations, and loudspeaker systems enable railway staff to keep passengers informed not only at the stations but also on the trains. This is another idea that railways have copied from the airlines.

High speed trains (HSTs) are the railways' answer to competition from airlines for passenger traffic. No train can travel as fast as a jet airliner, but in densely-populated places like Western Europe and Japan some HSTs come close to matching air travel times between major cities. This is because they deliver passengers to city centres. On some flights, the time taken between the city centre and the airport is longer than the flight itself.

France and Japan are the two countries which have been most successful with HSTs. Their HSTs run on specially-built tracks with as few curves and gradients as possible so that trains do not have to slow down. The HSTs do not have to fit in with slower-moving traffic because no other trains use their tracks.

Japan's *Shinkansen* or 'Bullet Train' between Tokyo and Osaka, travelling at up to 210 kph, was the first HST line, opened in 1964. Since then, more *Shinkansen* lines have been built. They are powered by electricity from overhead wires. A central control system allows the trains to run at high speeds in complete safety. There are no

signals on the line. Instead, the control room tells the driver how fast he should be travelling.

French HSTs are called TGVs (*Trains à Grandes Vitesses*). The first TGV line opened between Paris and Lyons in 1981 and cut the rail journey time between the two cities from nearly four hours to exactly two, beating the flight time. TGVs regularly reach 275 kph and have travelled at over 400 kph.

In other countries HSTs use existing tracks. This is partly because of the cost of building new lines and partly because in many places there is simply no space for extra tracks. Even with modern electronic signalling and track alterations to straighten out curves, HSTs running on existing track cannot match the speeds of the *Shinkansen* and TGVs, but they give greatly improved journey times. For example, the 640 km trip between London and Glasgow, which used to take five hours, has been cut to four by HSTs travelling at an average speed of 160 kph. This is only 50 minutes longer than by air.

In the USA and Australia, where major cities are further apart, HSTs can never hope to match flight times. But in many other countries HSTs have won passengers back from the airlines and given rail travel new life.

Below A *Shinkansen Hikari* train crossing the Fuji River with the slopes of the volcano Fuji-san in the background. The traction system is electric, and there is a motor to each axle of the train, giving rapid acceleration and a smooth ride. Much of the southern part of the journey passes through tunnels.

Under the city

There are about 100 cities throughout the world which already have underground railway systems or are planning to build one. Putting railways underground avoids using costly city building land and takes traffic away from busy city streets. Almost all underground lines are for passenger traffic only, but one exception is a special line across central London which carries mail between sorting offices. This adds to the efficiency of the postal services.

There are two ways of building railways underground. One is to bore a tunnel which runs deep under the buildings, streets and rivers. The other method is called 'cut and cover'. It involves digging a trench, building a tunnel inside it and then replacing earth over the top. Today, it is difficult to find enough open spaces inside cities for 'cut and cover' building and new underground railways are almost always deep-bored.

The Washington DC subway is a new rapid transit system designed to carry one million or more passengers each day. The trains are computer-controlled by a system which starts and stops them at the stations, controls the speed and opens and closes the doors. Much of the system runs underground.

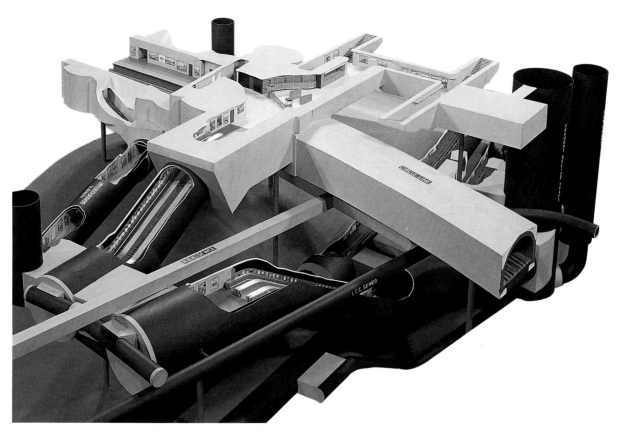

This model of a small part of the London Underground system shows how much tunnelling was necessary to create the complicated network. Beneath the city streets there is a rabbit warren of escalators, platforms, ticket halls, track and also the main sewage system for the city.

An underground railway is designed to move large numbers of people from one place to another quickly. Coaches have wide automatic doors and wide gangways so that they can be filled or emptied fast. The stations, too, must be carefully designed. Large entrance halls, wide corridors, ticket-issuing machines and escalators all help people to move quickly through them. All modern underground systems use electric traction to avoid polluting the air, and as space is restricted they take their electricity from conductor rails. Although the trains are pollution-free, ventilation and air conditioning in the tunnels and at stations are important for passenger health and comfort, particularly at rush hours.

At a city centre station, in the morning and evening rush hours, trains often follow each other at intervals of two minutes or less. This means that signalling systems must be precise. Block signalling using track circuits, controlled from a central control room, allows lines to be very heavily used.

A breakdown on an underground system can quickly cause chaos right across a city, and for this reason the servicing and maintenance of trains and track is a vitally important part of an underground operation. Most of this is done during the few hours each night when the system is closed down.

Because there are so many stops, travel by underground is fairly slow. In Paris, this has been overcome by building a separate 'express' system with fewer stops in the city centre.

New systems for the city

Throughout the world, cities continue to grow in size and their road traffic problems increase. This has forced many cities to look again at rapid transit systems for moving people about. For some, underground railways are the answer, but they are expensive to build.

One solution is to build elevated railways above street level. Germany has been one of the leaders in the use of elevated lines. Some of these are monorails – systems using only one line. One famous line between the West German towns of Wuppertal and Sonnborn, opened in 1901, has coaches suspended below its single rail. Another monorail elevated track carries visitors round Disneyland in California.

Above An overhead monorail system at the World Fair in Vancouver, Canada.
Below The new light railway recently developed in London's dockland.

The Wuppertal overhead railway, opened in 1901, is the world's oldest monorail.

Elevated lines are cheaper to build than underground ones, but they are still costly and many people think they are unsightly. Many cities have now built or are planning systems using light rapid transit vehicles (LRTVs). Some of these systems are built on the surface, often alongside roads. Others run for short distances underground in city centres and rise to the surface in less built-up areas.

LRTVs are cheaper to build and operate than ordinary trains, and because they are lighter they can use track which is cheaper to lay.

Another idea for rapid transit in cities is to bring back trams, which were once a major means of transport in cities. Trams which used tracks laid in the streets were scrapped because they caused hold-ups for other road traffic, but recently people have come to see that they had many advantages. They used very little energy, and as they were powered by electricity they caused no pollution. The problem of holding up other traffic can be solved by building separate tram tracks alongside roads, and some cities have started systems of this kind. Perhaps, one day, someone will think of a useful word to describe these systems which are partly tramways and partly light railways.

Outside cities, rapid transit systems such as monorails and LRTVs are often used for fairly short journeys between one place and another, such as between a city centre and an airport (as in Tokyo) or even between a main-line railway station and an airport departure terminal (as at London Gatwick Airport). As there are no stops between the beginning and the end of the line such services can provide very fast journeys.

Even the most powerful ordinary locomotive cannot climb gradients steeper than about 1 in 14. Its wheels cannot grip the rails and simply spin round. Ordinary railways built in mountainous areas like the Rockies in North America or the Alps in Europe have to climb slowly through long curves or tunnel through the mountains. But sometimes steep gradients cannot be avoided, and special mountain railways are built.

There are two types of mountain railway. One uses a traction system called rack and pinion. The rack is a toothed rail or a kind of ladder built between the rails or to one side of them. The pinion is a cog-wheel whose teeth slot into the rack, and this action pulls the train along. If the train comes to a halt on the slope, the rack and pinion prevent it from slipping.

The first rack and pinion railway was built in 1869 in the USA and is still in use. It carries passengers up Mount Washington in New Hampshire. Two years later, Europe's first rack and pinion railway was opened in Switzerland, and it was followed by many more. The first lines had gradients no steeper than 1 in 5, but a Swiss engineer, Edouard Locher, invented a double rack and pinion system which could hold trains on a slope as steep as 1 in 2.

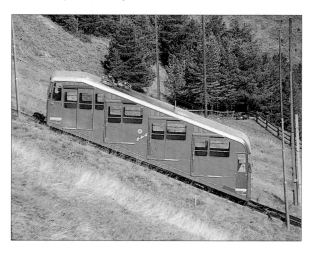

Above A rack and pinion railway climbs the mountain at St Moritz, Switzerland. It is powered by overhead electricity.

Conventional rail

Pinion wheel

Rack (third toothed rail)

Left The toothed rail of a rack and pinion railway prevents the train from slipping and from rolling backwards. The pinion acts as the driving wheel and is connected to an electric motor.

Rack and pinion railways are usually only a few kilometres long, and most of them are used to carry tourists. The trains travel slowly, usually at speeds of about 10 kph. Most mountain railways are operated by electric locomotives, but the Mount Washington railway and the Snowdon Mountain Railway in North Wales are both operated by steam.

The second type of mountain railway has coaches connected by cable to a stationary engine at the top. These are called funicular or cable railways. There are usually two tracks, with a cable car on each. As one car ascends the slope, the other descends. In this way, most of the power needed to pull one coach up is provided by the force of gravity acting on the other. Sometimes the cars have water tanks which can be filled to increase their weight for the downward journey. If the cable slips or snaps, an automatic brake stops the cars.

Cable railways can be operated only if the route is straight, and they are used for short climbs. In Britain, a number of seaside towns built on cliffs have cable railways for visitors.

This cable car takes winter sports passengers to the summit of a peak in the Swiss Alps. The car is connected by cable to a powerful winding motor at the top.

Before the railway age, the fastest anyone on earth had ever travelled was on a racehorse, at a speed of about 40 kph. In 1829 one of the first steam locomotives, the *Rocket*, reached over 46 kph, and from then on train speeds crept up and up. Within twenty years regular services were running at over 80 kph. By the 1870s the journey from London to Manchester, just over 300 km, took 4 hours 15 minutes. Fifty years before, by stage coach, it had taken 20 hours.

Railways all over the world were proud of the speed of their services, and still are, but there was another reason for developing faster locomotives. The faster trains run, the more trains can use a line, and so the more business the railway can do. Better engineering design and developments like compounding and super-heating increased both the speed and the pulling power of steam locomotives until, in 1938, the British *Mallard* achieved the speed of 202.7 kph. This is still the world speed record for steam.

At Lucerne in Switzerland this old steam engine was renovated and brought out during the 100 year celebrations of the local railway.

Alongside each other are two generations of famous steam locomotives. The A4 Pacific 4498, *Sir Nigel Gresley* (left) was named after the designer of the Pacific class. This included *Mallard*, which in 1938 became the fastest steam locomotive with a speed of over 200 kph. The Hardwicke racer No 790 (right) achieved a speed of 130 kph in the 1890s.

Electric traction and the smooth running of HST lines have enabled the overall speed record for a train to be pushed to 409 kph. This was reached by a French TGV train in 1988.

It was not only in locomotive-building that the railways discovered and developed new technologies. Before the railways arrived, very few tunnels had been built, and bridges needed only to carry the weight of horse-drawn vehicles. Cuttings and embankments involved moving earth on a scale that had never been known before. Solving the problems of railway-building created the science of civil engineering which has given us today's fast highways. Even road traffic lights were developed from ideas that the railways had pioneered.

WORLD RECORDS

The longest railway   The Trans-Siberian Railway (Moscow to Vladivostok), 9,654 km.

The longest straight stretch of track The Nullarbor Straight, Western and South Australia, 478 km.

The longest railway tunnel   The Seikan Tunnel between Honshu and Hokkaido, Japan, 54 km.

The largest railway system   USA, 319,000 km.

The fastest steam locomotive   Mallard (UK), 1938, 202.7 kph.

The fastest train   TGV Sud-Est, France, 1988, 409 kph.

The French TGV high speed train holds the world speed record at 409 kph, which it achieved in 1988. This was about twice the speed achieved by the steam locomotive *Mallard* 50 years previously.

There are two things that railways can do better than any other form of transport. They can move large numbers of people quickly into and out of cities, and they can move large amounts of heavy, bulky freight. These two activities will continue to be the most important jobs the railways do.

In densely-populated parts of the world such as Western Europe, the building of more HST lines, or the improvement of tracks so that they can take HSTs, will continue to provide competition with the airlines for long-distance passenger business. There are already plans for an HST line, modelled on the French TGV system, from Moscow to Leningrad in the USSR. France, which has always been keen on railways, now leads the world in the design of HSTs and the operation of HST systems. A French company has been set up in the USA to look into possible HST routes there.

The railways of Western Europe will receive a boost when the HST rail tunnel under the English Channel between Britain and France, with trains running at up to 300 kph, opens in the 1990s. Meanwhile, more and more traffic-choked cities all over the world are likely to turn to LRTVs to persuade people to leave their cars at home and travel by train.

By 1993 there will be a two-way rail tunnel, about 50 km long, between England and France. Trains will be able to carry passengers between London and Paris in about three hours. This model shows the Eurotunnel terminal at Folkestone, Kent. Here, cars and trucks will be able to drive on and off shuttle trains, and there will be a similar terminal at Calais in France.

In the future most large cities will need to have rapid transit systems for carrying people from one side of a city to the other. This overhead railway at Ueno Park, Tokyo, is one type of system that many cities would be able to establish.

One problem that the railways have not yet solved is that of noise. HSTs cause disturbance to people living hundreds of metres from the track. As the number of HST lines grows, it is likely that people will demand that they are put underground where they pass through built-up areas or near tourist attractions. This will greatly increase the cost of building new lines, but it may be that railways will get permission to build only if they agree. Already, the newest TGV lines in northern France are being built with tunnels and embankments to cut down noise along part of their routes.

After about 20 years during which it seemed that railways were doomed, people – and, more important, governments – have come to see that they still have an important job to do. People are travelling more, whether on business or for pleasure. There are still many countries in the world where there are few cars and the only way to travel is by rail. No one knows what rail travel will be like in a hundred years' time – but it is certain that the method of transport that began in 1825, when the very first train set out on the 20-kilometre journey from Darlington to Stockton, will still be running.

Glossary

Air brakes. System which uses the force of compressed air to push the brake shoes into contact with the wheels.

Automatic train control. System which warns the driver of a train when approaching a danger signal.

Ballast. Chippings used as a foundation for railway track.

Block. Length of track controlled by a signal.

Civil engineering. Planning and designing large structures such as roads, railways, bridges and tunnels.

Commuter. Someone who travels to work each day.

Compound locomotive. Locomotive which uses steam twice before expelling it through the funnel.

Compressed air. Air at a pressure greater than atmospheric pressure.

Cutting. A gap cut through high ground to avoid a slope.

Destination. The place where a train is going.

Electromagnet. Magnet which works when an electric current is passed through it.

Elevated railway. Railway built on columns and carried above street level.

Escalator. Moving staircase.

Fare. The money paid for a journey.

Friction. The resistance of one object to another moving over it.

Funicular railway. Cable railway.

Gangway. Passage between seats.

Gradient. Slope.

HST. High Speed Train.

Hump. A slope in a marshalling yard which slows wagons down so that they can be uncoupled.

Interlocking. System which links points with signals so that one cannot be changed without the other.

Junction. Place where two or more railway tracks join.

LRTV. Light Rapid Transit Vehicle.

Maglev. Train following a magnetic track.

Maintenance. Keeping equipment in good running order.

Marshalling yard. Sidings where freight trains are split up and new trains are formed.

Monorail. Single rail.

Pantograph. Metal frame on top of a traction unit which collects electricity from overhead wires.

Parlour car. Luxury passenger coach.

Paved Concrete Track (PACT). Track laid direct on to a base of reinforced concrete.

Points. A set of rails which can be switched to move a train to a different line.

Pollution. Spoiling the environment by, for example, smoke or noise.

Punctual. On time.

Railcar. Single coach with a built-in traction unit.

Relay. Switch which works when an electric current passes through it.

Rush hours. Busy times in the morning and evening when commuters are travelling to or from work.

Safety valve. Tap which allows steam to escape from a steam engine if the pressure is too high.

Shinkansen. Japanese high speed train.

Superheating. Heating steam after it has been made to increase the amount of work a locomotive can do.

Telegraph. System for sending messages by wire.

TGV. *Trains à Grandes Vitesses* — French high speed trains.

Transcontinental. From one side of a continent to the other.

Turbine. Engine which produces power when oil, steam, water or gas pass through the slots of a wheel and make it turn.

Turbo-train. Train powered by a turbine locomotive.

Vacuum brake. System that uses a vacuum — the absence of air — to operate brake shoes.

Viaduct. Structure like a bridge that carries a road or railway across a valley.

Weld. Join metal together with molten metal.

Further reading

Carter, E.F., *Famous Railway Stations of the World and Their Traffic* (Frederick Muller 1958)

Cowie, L.W., *The Railway Age* (Macdonald 1978)

Griswold, Wesley S., *Work of Giants: building the first transcontinental railroad* (Frederick Muller 1963)

Hollingsworth, Brian and Cook, Arthur, *Modern Locomotives* (Salamander Books 1983)

Hollingsworth, Brian and Cook, Arthur, *The World's Steam Passenger Locomotives* (Salamander Books 1981)

Jane's World Railways (Jane's Yearbooks published annually)

Marshall, John, *Guinness Book of Rail Facts and Feats* (Guinness Superlatives 1971)

Nock, O. S., *Encyclopedia of Railways* (Octopus 1977)

Nock, O. S., *The Railway Enthusiast's Encyclopedia* (Hutchinson 1968)

Nock, O. S., *World Atlas of Railways* (Victoria House 1978)

Whitehouse, P. B., *Great Trains of the World* (Hamlyn 1975)

Wood, Sydney, *The Railway Revolution* (Macmillan 1981)

Picture acknowledgements

The publishers would like to thank the following for allowing their photographs to be reproduced in this book:
Alison Anholt-White 21 (above); Eurotunnel 42; Hutchison 4; Picturepoint (cover); Topham 6, 10, 15 (both), 25 (right), 29, 30, 31 (below), 35, 36, 38, 39, 40, 41 (below); TRH (The Research House) 5 (above), 26, 34; ZEFA 5 (below), 7, 8, 11, 13, 14, 17, 19 (both), 20, 23, 24, 25 (left), 31 (above), 32, 36, 37, 41 (above), 43.
Artwork by Nick Hawken.

Index